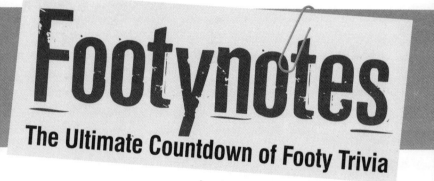

Footynotes

The Ultimate Countdown of Footy Trivia

Footynotes

The Ultimate Countdown of Footy Trivia

By
Chris Kamara and **Richard Digance**

This edition first published in the UK in 2008 By Green Umbrella Publishing

© Green Umbrella Publishing 2008

www.gupublishing.co.uk

Publishers: Jules Gammond and Vanessa Gardner

Creative Director: Kevin Gardner

Picture Credits: Nigel Ferris Photography and Shutterstock

Robert Segal Representation

Printed and bound by J. H. Haynes & Co. Ltd., Sparkford

ISBN: 978-1-906635-16-9

Footynotes

The Ultimate Countdown of Footy Trivia

By
Chris Kamara and Richard Digance

GreenUmbrella
Publishing

Footynotes

Contents

Footynotes

Kammy and Digance

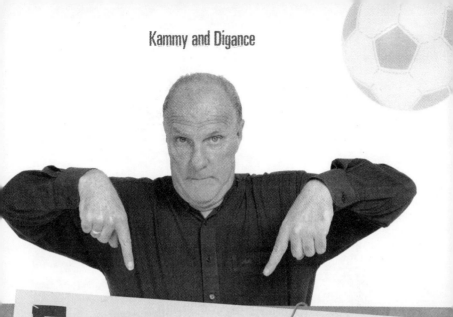

Footynotes

The Ultimate Countdown of Footy Trivia

Footynotes   9

Players bits and pieces

David Seaman captained England in just one international

Footynote: The only England captain to wear a pony tail

Dion Dublin broke his neck playing for Sheffield Wednesday in 1999

Footynote: Past *Countdown* fans may wish to know Sheffield Wednesday is the only football club made up of two nine letter words

By the way, Manchester City goalkeeper Bert Trautmann who also broke his neck in the 1956 FA Cup final was court martialled in 1945 after being captured by the Russians

Footynote: Other than that Bert led a quiet life

Fernando Torres is a huge fan of *Lord of the Rings*

Footynote: He read the book once and then made a hobbit of it

Scott Parker featured in a McDonalds ad when he was a kid

Footynote: We wonder if John Hartson and Jan Molby were standing in the queue?

Peter Osgood slept with the FA Cup

Footynote: We don't think the FA Cup was married though

Ryan Giggs was the first footballer to be mentioned in *The Simpsons*

Footynote: Followed by Pelé, Ronaldo and Beckham

Emile Heskey's middle name is Ivanhoe

Footynote; His mother must have had a knight to remember

Frank Lampard went to public school

Footynote; He also went on loan to Swansea from West Ham so swings and roundabouts Frank

Footynotes

Paul Ince's full name is Paul Emerson Carlyle Ince

Footynote; Didn't Emerson Carlyle play for Brazil?

Eric Cantona played the part of a French Diplomat in the 1998 movie *Elizabeth*

Footynote; Is that the one where he drop-kicked Sir Francis Drake for winning at bowls Kammy?

Alan Curbishley's middle name is Llewellyn

Footynote; Good East End of London name

When David Beckham joined Manchester United Ryan Giggs sold him a Ford Escort

Footynote; Hmm, Becks and an Escort rings a bell Kammy

Footynotes

Ryan Giggs played for Manchester City before he played for Manchester United

Footynote: And England schoolboys before he played for Wales, a man of options

Mark Hughes won four FA Cup Winner's medals

Footynote: Kammy claims Sparky was the toughest player he ever marked. And when he says marked he means marked

Mark Hughes' actual name is Leslie

Footynote: So Mark was an order and not a name then?

Owen Hargreaves was born in Calgary, played for England and had a residential qualification to play for Germany

Footynote: That's what we used to call in the old days a gypsy

Steven Gerrard once had a trial with Manchester United as did John Terry

Footynote: Did Manchester United miss the point of trials then?

Footynotes

Kammy and Digance

Footynotes

Andriy Shevchenko won a pair of Ian Rush's boots when he was 14

Footynote; He didn't take them to Chelsea with him

Tommy Docherty once said of Dwight Yorke that if he became a top player then Docherty's name was Mao Tse Tung

Footynote; Well, his name is an anagram of Red Ty Cho which translated into native American means Big Foot In Mouth

Matthew Le Tissier once wrongly stated that Kanu of Portsmouth wore size 25 boots

Footynote; That really would have confirmed Kanu as a canoe

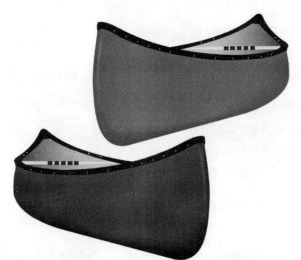

Kevin Davies of Bolton Wanderers committed the most fouls in the 2006-07 Premiership season

Footynote; A striker in both senses of the word

In 1986 David Beckham was the Manchester United mascot in a match against West Ham

Footynote; So who held his hand when he walked on the pitch? Or didn't they do that then?

José Mourinho was arrested for smuggling a dog into Britain in 2007

Footynote; Why do we keep thinking of hotel rooms here?

George Best was rejected by Irish club Glentoran for being too small

Footynote; Surely not in the land of leprechauns?

Jamie Redknapp began his career with Bournemouth

Footynote; And his dad Harry ended his playing career at the same place

Jamie Redknapp and Frank Lampard are cousins

Footynote: Then they must never marry

Sol Campbell's actual name is Sulzeer

Footynote: But you won't get away with it in Scrabble

By the way, speaking of Scrabble, Albert Quixall was a record signing when he joined Manchester United from Sheffield Wednesday in 1958 for £45,000

Footynote: Kammy was part of the exchange deal

Footynotes

French international and now football pundit Marcel Desailly was actually born in Ghana

Footynote: John Motson was born in Salford, Lancashire

Andy Goram played both football and cricket for Scotland

Footynote: And he too was born in Lancashire, in Bury

Arsenal signed goalkeeper Richard Wright for £6 million and he played 12 times

Footynote: That's about 50 grand a save or 47 grand per goal kick

Manchester United goalkeeper Peter Schmeichel is an accomplished pianist

Footynote: And Pavarotti was a slightly less accomplished keeper and Juventus fan

Zinedine Zidane was given 14 red cards in his career

Footynote: And in his last game he really was ZZ Topper

England goalkeeper David Seaman once injured himself reaching for his TV remote

Footynote; Probably dropped it

Another England goalkeeper Peter Bonnetti became a postman in Scotland for a while

Footynote; He must have enjoyed himself between the posts

Yet another England goalkeeper David James collects mountain bikes

Footynote; Should have given one to Peter Bonnetti when he became a postman

David James has played for six different Premiership clubs

Footynote; And still counting

Michael Owen has a golf handicap of eight

Footynote; He has a good collection of clubs!

Kevin Keegan's real name is Joseph

Footynote; So he changed to Kevin because........er because.....it was easier to spell than ....er Joe?

Pelé's real name is Edson Arantes do Nascimento

Footynote: Joe we would have understood

David Beckham played on loan with Preston North End

Footynote: Shame he didn't come up to their expectations

Bobby Charlton managed Preston North End

Footynote: So did Nobby Stiles.....were they making their way through the 1966 side?

Joe Cole's football hero was Vinnie Jones

Footynote: Vinnie's football hero was Rocky

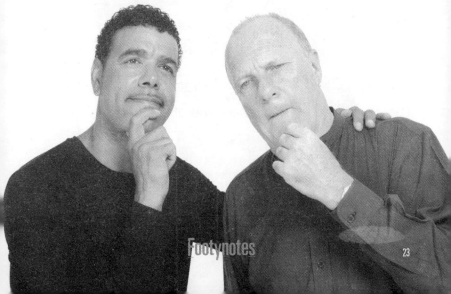

Footynotes

Russian Andrei Arshavin has a degree in fashion design

Footynote; That's how he skirts round defenders

Robert Earnshaw's mother was a professional boxer

Footynote; Oh no, not the Labrador gag…..no, we like Rob

Liverpool's Robbie Keane's father was a rock singer

Footynote; So was Mick Jagger's daughter's father

Footynotes

Aleksander Hleb's mother was a bricklayer

Footnote; That's probably who taught him to get round a wall then

Cristiano Ronaldo's full name is Cristiano Ronaldo dos Santos Aveiro

Footnote; Need a big contract to get the whole name on

He was called Ronaldo because his father's favourite actor was Ronald Reagan

Footnote; Luckily it wasn't John Wayne. Johnno sounds more Sunday League, less Champions League

Pope John Paul II played in goal in the Polish League

Footnote; Very much Hands of God

Steven Gerrard's middle name is George

Footnote; Cue the racehorse Stevie GG

Real Madrid legend Alfredo di Stefano played for three different countries, Argentina, Spain and Columbia

Footnote; So where was he born?

Footynotes

David Beckham was literally given the boot by Sir Alex Ferguson on 15th February 2003 when he kicked a boot at his player after being knocked out of the cup by Arsenal

Footynote: That boot has allegedly appeared on ebay four million times we think

Leeds and England's David Batty was once run over by his daughter on his bike

Footynote: She could have been 25 and the bike could have been a Harley Davidson so he should consider himself lucky

Who scored and when

Footynote: A reference of course to goals and nothing else

Some goals are scored and some goals are missed
Which means either strikers or keepers are kissed
Which is why in this poem we can confide
Some strikers on purpose kick the ball wide

It's ok to train with your team-mates and go jogging
But quite frankly there's some just not into snogging
So now you know that's why some of them miss
They'd rather do that than have a slobbery kiss

The first ever Premiership goal was scored in 1992 by Brian Deane for Sheffield United against Manchester United

Footynote: Nothing to do with anything and completely irrelevant but Brian Deane is an anagram of "need a brain"

In a game between Arsenal and Aston Villa in 1935 Arsenal's Ted Drake scored two hat-tricks in their 7-1 victory

Footynote; Don't Drakes score ducks?

In November 1968 referee Ivan Robinson scored for Barrow against Plymouth Argyle due to a wicked deflection

Footynote; Rumour has it he was Barrow's leading scorer that season

Bryan Robson scored for England after just 27 seconds

Footynote; But he is still the only man to break his collar-bone on *Question of Sport*

Footynotes

Goalkeeper Alex Stepney of Manchester United scored two penalties in 1975

Footynote: Nobody had the heart to tell him that wasn't his job

In 1936 Joe Payne of Luton Town scored 10 goals in one game against Bristol Rovers

Footynote: So to Bristol Rovers fans he was a Payne in the backside

On making his debut for Stoke City in 1979 Brendan O'Callaghan scored after just 10 seconds

Footynote: We hope he scored for Stoke or it wasn't a great debut

In 1908 Newcastle were playing Sunderland. Half time score was 1-1 but Sunderland scored eight goals in 28 minutes and won 9-1

Footynote: We assume they checked the oranges for drugs?

In 1984 Stirling beat Selkirk 20-0 in a Scottish cup-tie of which David Thompson scored seven

Footynote; Selkirk's manager may have accepted the 10-0-0 formation didn't really work

When Portsmouth beat Reading 7-4 on September 30th 2007 it was the highest score in a top league game since 1958 when Tottenham beat Everton 10-4

Footynote; Yeah but Portsmouth would never win the FA Cup for as long as......(whoops)

When the German ladies side won the World Cup in 2007, beating Brazil 2-0 they became the only side to go through the entire tournament without conceding a goal

Footynote; Or shaving? Which is not applicable to a Brazilian

The first ever penalty was scored for Wolverhampton Wanderers by John Heath in 1891 against Accrington Stanley

Footynote; Stanley of Accrington must have been a dirty player

Gary Lineker scored 10 World Cup goals for England

Footynote; He bagged them and hit 'em crisp

Gary Lineker scored a goal every 1.7 games for England and was never booked in his 17 year career

Footynote; Kammy was booked every 1.7 games and never played for England in his 22 year career

Paulino Alcantara scored 356 goals for Barcelona

Footynote; So how come he's not famous then?

Toré Andre Flo scored a hat-trick for Chelsea against Barcelona in 2000

Footynote; Wasn't he the bloke who made Peter Crouch look like Ronnie Corbett?

David Beckham hit the net against Wimbledon from the halfway line in 1996

Footynote; Surely if it hit the net at Wimbledon it didn't count then?

Goal difference came into play for the first time in 1976

Footynote; Until then we assume all goals looked the same. Two posts and a crossbar

Dixie Dean scored a hat-trick for England against Belgium in 1927 and another against Luxembourg 10 days later

Footynote; Come back Dixie, England needs you

Between 1927 and 1932 Dixie Dean scored more England goals than he made appearances, scoring 18 times in 16 games

Footynote; By the way, Dixie hated being called Dixie, his real name was Bill. Kammy hated some of the names he was called too

The above fact was bettered by the lesser known George Camsell of Middlesbrough

Footynotes

who scored 18 goals in nine games
from 1929

Footynote; Kammy made 12 of them

Dixie Dean scored in his first five England
internationals

Footynote; Kammy didn't

George Best was Manchester United's
leading scorer for five successive seasons

Footynote; In more ways than one….nice one George

Rogerio Ceni the Sao Paulo goalkeeper has scored 72 goals from 44 free kicks and 28 penalties

Footynote; And they still haven't realised he's not playing in his best position

In 1963 Sporting Lisbon beat Apoel Nicosia 16-1 in the European Club competition

Footynote; Not actually that sporting at all if you want our opinion

Striker Tony Cottee of West Ham played for England seven times and never scored an international goal

Footynote; Kammy never played for England and he never scored an international goal either

In September 1885 Arbroath beat Bon Accord 36-0 in the Scottish Cup but what isn't generally known is that Bon Accord were actually a cricket team and their goalkeeper had never played before

Footynote; Or ever again we reckon

On the same day as the above game Dundee Harp beat Aberdeen Rovers 35-0

Footynote: We reckon the goals of the day TV programme would have run for two days

When England beat Northern Ireland 13-0 in 1882 Aston Villa's Howard Vaughton scored five on his debut and his Villa team-mate Arthur Brown scored four

Footynote: Arthur Brown? Wasn't that two and sixpence in old money or was that half a crown?

In a game between Aston Villa and Leicester in 1976 Chris Nicholl scored all four goals in a 2-2 draw

Footynote; He was determined to get man of the match whoever won

The 1980 Asia Cup final between Hong Kong and North Korea was decided on penalties… 28 of them….the final score was 11-10

Footynote; Did North Korea's players' boots have "made round the corner" stamped on them?

Sir Geoff Hurst scored six goals against Sunderland

Footynote; And they knighted him for that????

By the way, Geoff Hurst also played one first class cricket match for Essex in 1962

Footynote; He'd have played a lot more if he hadn't headed the ball to silly mid on

In the 1960 European Cup final between Real Madrid and Eintracht, Madrid's Ferenc Puskas scored four goals and Alfredo di

Footynotes

Stefano scored three in the 7-3 victory

Footynote: Goal-hangers no doubt?

In 1956 Huddersfield Town, managed by Bill Shankly, drew 6-6 with Charlton Athletic

Footynote: So both clubs bought goalkeepers in 1957?

On the subject of Huddersfield and Charlton, the following year Charlton were winning 5-1 with 30 minutes to go. The final score was 7-6 to Charlton

Footynote: Wrong about the goalkeepers then

In 1890 Jack Reynolds scored for both England and Ireland. He played for both

Footynote: That must have done everyone's brains in. Or was that Jack Daniels?

Footynotes

In 1950 Stan Mortensen of Blackpool scored England's first ever goal in the World Cup finals against Chile

Footynote; Too hot for Chile eh?

Willie Hall of Tottenham scored five goals for England against Ireland in 1938. Three of them were scored in three and a half minutes

Footynote; Wonder if Ireland had gone off for half time

Johnny Byrne, originally of Crystal Palace, scored six goals in his first three internationals in 1964 but was never chosen again after 1965

Footynote; Even when you score you sometimes don't get anywhere

In a Second Division game between Crystal Palace and Brighton the referee Kelvin Morton awarded five penalties yet Palace won 2-1

Footynote; Sounds like a few prospective England penalty takers in that game

Footynotes

Matthew Taylor, playing for Portsmouth, scored with a 42 yard volley in 2006

Footynote: Kammy was there and he reckons he hit it from the car park

Although Robbie Fowler was left-footed he scored 31 goals with his right foot by the time he joined Cardiff City

Footynote: Which means he allegedly owns more houses than he has scored goals with his right foot

Pelé's 1,000th goal was a penalty for Santos in his 909th game in 1960

Footynote: Kammy has reviewed the incident and reckons the penalty should never have been given. Spoil-sport

Tommy Hutchison of Manchester City scored for both sides in the 1981 FA Cup final against Tottenham Hotspur

Footynote: He was determined to get a winner's medal whichever side won

Footygrams – players

Try these anagrams out with your pals. Assuming we all
have one dodgy mate we've made the first one or two
very easy:

When a word is very young
Its letters number perhaps just one
Like I and A and then it's two
Like me, my, go and do
Then cat and dog and up to three
That's how a big word comes to be
And so we jumble letters around
And we see the growth in them
Until they became the name of a football team
Like HeartofMidlothian

Peel – **Pelé**

O never share wag – **Owen Hargreaves**

Top level spec – **Steve Coppell**

Sell us a chop – **Paul Scholes**

Brigadier Dod – **Didier Drogba**

A deep prank Jim – **Jamie Redknapp**

A hen pill – **Phil Neal**

Learn a share – **Alan Shearer**

Bless in Toby – **Nobby Stiles**

Green Hog Coe – **George Cohen**

Eg Get sober – **George Best**

Curves beet – **Steve Bruce**

Ah welcome in – **Michael Owen**

Dry Ron shame – **Rodney Marsh**

Oil West Ham nil – **Lewis Hamilton** (crafty one)

False Mary – **Alf Ramsey**

Drive van son – **Viv Anderson**

Nobby Dills – **Billy Bonds**

A hand stone – **Dean Ashton**

Idled by a vent – **David Bentley**

Inside news – **Dennis Wise**

Coronation lad sir – **Cristiano Ronaldo**

Friend or a nid – **Rio Ferdinand**

Yen wag bride – **Wayne Bridge**

Tin ocean car – **Eric Cantona**

As moth went up – **Matthew Upson**

Yer magic ball – **Craig Bellamy**

Footynotes

Arc I am shark – **Chris Kamara**

And my very – **Mervyn Day**

Oh grunter! – **Roger Hunt**

Sprint a metre – **Martin Peters**

Watt the cool – **Theo Walcott**

Tot wealth co – **Theo Walcott**

Row ye anyone – **Wayne Rooney**

Self jet fling – **Jeff Stelling**

Nb la la la – **Alan Ball**

Sue go a placing – **Paul Gascoigne**

Un Plaice – **Paul Ince**

Miln relation – **Martin O'Neill**

Are greens new – **Arsene Wenger**

Evening kake – **Kevin Keegan**

Farmlands nr park – **Frank Lampard Snr**

Hector Pruce – **Peter Crouch**

LN tops either – **Peter Shilton**

Of tiny men – **Tom Finney**

Peers banter – **Peter Barnes**

Ry sagging – **Ryan Giggs**

JD save maid – **David James**

Nob fester – **Ben Foster**

Oh AJ shone – **John O'Shea**

Retry John – **John Terry**

Footynotes

I raw thing – Ian Wright

Please her – Lee Sharpe

Get a heart sought – Gareth Southgate

Ye shaving – Shay Given

Only gate – Tony Gale

Missile tatter – Matt Le Tissier

JND owns a heron – Andrew Johnson

O grand bonks – Gordon Banks

Neat crumbs – Marcus Bent

Wary in silk – Ray Wilkins

Born by boobs – Bobby Robson

Players bits and pieces of years ago

Porky was a pig who wasn't very big
But he was not forsaken cos he wasn't that much bacon
What has this to do with a football book?
It's just coming up, take a look

In 1995, an Indonesian player Mistar was killed by a herd of pigs that invaded the pitch

Footynote: And we are not telling porkies

Lal Hilditch was the only player-manager of Manchester United in 1927

Footynote: He left when he couldn't agree terms with himself

Jurgen Klinsmann joined Tottenham Hotspur twice, once in 1994 and again in 1997

Footynote: He even left his towel on the massage bed

Cobi Jones of the USA and ex-Coventry City was the youngest player to reach 100 international caps at the age of 27 in 1998

Footynote: Not one of them fitted over his dreadlocks

Raymond Kopa of Real Madrid was the first footballer to receive the Legion of Honour in 1970

Footynote: So we guess he joined the Foreign Legion and was never seen again

Nat Lofthouse of Bolton Wanderers was still a coal miner when he played his first game for England

Footynote: The first footballing coke-freak then?

Arthur Wharton was the first black player in English football

Footnote; Hang on, if Nat Lofthouse was a coal miner....oh never mind

The first cash transfer was in 1893 when Jimmy Crabtree joined Aston Villa from Burnley

Footnote; Kammy still has the white fiver in his wallet

George Eastham was the first England player whose father also played for England

Footnote; Followed by Frank Lampard, Shaun Wright-Phillips and Nigel Clough, a great quiz question gang

Bill Foulkes of Manchester United played in a league game just two weeks after the Munich air disaster

Footnote; That's how tough centre halves used to be

Bobby Moore made his final England appearance on 4th November 1973 against Italy at Wembley. It was his 108th international

Footynotes

Footynote; His middle name was Chelsea by the way

Johnny Carey played in every position for Manchester United except outside left, including playing in goal against Sunderland in 1953

Footynote; Kammy must have had his work cut out marking him

Raich Carter is the only player to win an FA Cup medal either side of the Second World War

Footynote; Other players won medals between times though but for a very different and obvious reason

Sir Alf Ramsey said Martin Peters was 10 years ahead of his time

Footynote; So why didn't he play for England 10 years later?

Graeme Souness of Liverpool was born on 6th May 1954 the same day Roger Bannister broke the four minute mile

Footynote; Kammy used to run away from Graeme Souness on the pitch but not that quickly

Tom Finney, Preston North End and England legend, was never booked

Footnote: If Kammy had received one more booking in his career he would have received a telegram from the Queen

Pat Jennings was the first ever player to make 1,000 first class appearances

Footnote: Kammy was the first to make 1,000 second rate appearances. He claims to have made 1,000 first class appearances himself but train journeys don't count

Footynotes

David Jack of Arsenal managed Sunderland Greyhound Stadium during the Second World War

Footynote: Shouldn't he have been busy in Europe as the world went to the dogs?

Phil Neal captained England for one game

Footynote: Under Sven Goran Eriksson England had several captains in just one game so Phil did well to keep hold of the armband that long

Chris Kamara signed Chris Waddle from Falkirk

Footynote: Kammy sent his scout for a report when manager of Bradford City and the report said "he can play a bit" Kammy replied "I know that, what's his fitness like you idiot"

In 2000 Sheffield Wednesday goalkeeper Kevin Pressman was sent off after just 13 seconds

Footynote: Kammy made him man of the match

Diego Maradona first came to Europe to play for Napoli

Footynote; Someone gave him a hand to get there

In a youth tournament in 1954 playing for Baura Athletic Club Pelé scored 148 goals in 33 games

Footynote; In a Middlesbrough youth tournament Kammy scored one goal in 9,000 games

Stanley Matthews was the first ever Footballer of the Year in 1948

Footynote; Kammy came second in 1947

Ephraim Longworth was the first Liverpool player to captain England in 1921

Footynote; Hey, with a name like that the guy deserved a break

Bobby Moore finished his career with the US side Seattle Sounders in 1978, playing seven games for them

Footynote; A great man who died on Richard Digance's birthday

Footynotes

Before he played for Leeds, Johnny Giles played on the wing at Manchester United

Footynote: Who for? Oh I see

Former Liverpool player Ray Houghton played in England, was born in Scotland and played for the Republic of Ireland

Footynote: So that's where Owen Hargreaves got the idea from

Former West Ham captain Billy Bonds loved bird-watching

Footynote: So did Stan Collymore

Elton John's uncle Roy Dwight played in an FA Cup final for Nottingham Forest against Luton Town and broke his leg

Footynote: It snapped like a candle in the wind

Martin Peters' middle name is Stanford

Footynote; A name 10 years ahead of its time

In 1939 goalkeeper Danny Bolton signed for Bolton Wanderers

Footynote; He thought it was the family run business

There have been eight pro footballers named Bolton but only the one wandered to the Wanderers

Footynote; Didn't one become a singer with dodgy hair?

Fred Blackburn played for Blackburn Rovers and England in 1902

Footynote; This is starting to get stupid

Footynotes

Tarquin Tottenham-Hotspur played for Spurs

Footynote: Now it is totally stupid....move on

1970s Norway international Svein Grondalen was badly injured when out jogging he collided with a moose

Footynote: Well, we've all collided with a few of them in our time eh?

Arsenal's Charlie George tragically cut off one of his toes with a lawn mower

Footynote: We remember Charlie's hairstyle and wonder if it was the same mower

In 1981 in a game between Plymouth and Chester, Chester keeper Grenville Millington crashed into a goalpost causing the goal to collapse. The game was abandoned

Footynote: The PFA allegedly sued the goalpost and lost

Another goalkeeper Chick Brodie of Brentford finished his career when a dog collided with him as he went to clear a ball upfield in a game against Colchester

Footynote; Obvious gag here about what she was doing on the pitch etc but we're not going there

Phil Thompson dropped the FA Cup in 1992 when it was presented to him

Footynote; He saw his reflection

Edward Stein of Barnet was the first black football manager

Footynote; Ahead of Keith Alexander, Viv Anderson and Kammy

Roberto Di Matteo manager of MK Dons scored the fastest ever Cup final goal for Chelsea in just 42 seconds

Footynote; It equalled Richard's personal best for 50 metre sprint

Johnny Haynes of Fulham was the first £100 per week player

Footynote: That won't even fill up the tank of a Range Rover nowadays

Dennis Wise has played in three FA Cup finals for three different clubs; Millwall, Chelsea and Wimbledon

Footynote: But has never been tall enough to collect a medal without standing on tiptoe

Dino Zoff is the oldest player to win the World Cup aged 40

Footynote: Anyone got Peter Shilton's phone number?

Scottish international Dave Mackay of Tottenham Hotspur broke his leg twice in the same 1963 season

Footynote: And remembering Dave Mackay as we do he probably didn't even notice

Playerfacts

David Beckham

When David Beckham went to Real Madrid,
At a cost of 25 million quid.
My granny said that was too much to pay,
She went to Spain for 75 quid in May.

Gran wants to tell David what a great time she had,
And in passing how much she fancies his dad.
She reckons David should do what she did,
And save himself 25 million quid.

From her room the view was almost a stunner,
Six days and all she spent was a oner.
There's a crochet room where everyone mingles,
And a family room two bunk beds, two singles.

It's not a hotel, nor a guesthouse as such,
You have to buy your own breakfast,

Footynotes

but it doesn't cost much.
They're building apartments each side of the place,
The waiter's Manuel and the food's a disgrace.

Apart from all that, my grandmother reckons,
It would have been the ideal spot for the Beckhams.
My gran thinks they would have been tempted to stay
And not cleared off to the US of A

Coming soon...............

George Best
Bobby Charlton
Brian Clough
Dixie Dean
Pelé
Roy Of The Rovers

George Best

Born in Belfast, Northern Ireland on 22nd May 1946, a football genius

Died on 25th November 2005 aged 59 and remembered forever as that football genius

George Best was discovered by football scout Bob Bishop who sent Matt Busby a telegram stating "I have found you a genius"

George Best was rejected by Irish club Glentoran for being too small

George Best never played in a World Cup tournament

George Best made his debut for Manchester United against West Bromwich Albion on 14th September 1963 at the age of 17

He played 466 games for Manchester United and scored 178 goals

Footynotes

He played 37 times for Northern Ireland

George scored nine goals for his country, four of these were against Cyprus

George Best was European Footballer of the Year in 1968

George Best was sacked by Manchester United at the age of 27

He won League Championship medals with Manchester United in 1965 and 1967

100,000 people attended his funeral in East Belfast

He is buried next to his mother Annie at Roselawn Cemetery, East Belfast

On 22nd May 2006 Belfast City Airport was re-named George Best Belfast City Airport

George Best played for Manchester United, Dunstable, Stockport County, Cork Celtic, Fulham, Los Angeles

Aztecs, Fort Lauderdale Strikers, Hibernian, San Jose Earthquakes, Bournemouth and the Brisbane Lions

Bobby Charlton

Bobby Charlton was born in Ashington, Northumberland on October 11th 1937

Bobby Charlton was the nephew of Newcastle United legend Jackie Milburn

Bobby Charlton was discovered by scout Joe Armstrong playing for East Northumberland Boys in 1953

Bobby Charlton played 759 games for Manchester United scoring 247 goals

Bobby Charlton once entered a TV quiz *Double Your Money* and answered questions on music

Bobby Charlton became manager of Preston North End for one season in 1973

Bobby Charlton did his National Service in Shrewsbury with Duncan Edwards

He made his debut for Manchester United against Charlton in 1956

His brother Jackie Charlton became a coal miner before he became a footballer

Bobby Charlton survived the Munich air disaster having swapped places with Tommy Taylor who was killed as the plane left Zemen Airport

Bobby Charlton was the first survivor to leave hospital

Bobby Charlton was European Footballer of the Year in 1966, the year he helped England win the World Cup

Bobby Charlton played for England 106 times until he was 32 and scored 49 goals

Bobby Charlton was knighted in 1994

Bobby Charlton for a while was a director of Wigan Athletic

Bobby Charlton played 31 games for Waterford United in 1975, scoring 18 goals

Bobby Charlton played his last game for Manchester United against Chelsea in 1973

Bobby Charlton was awarded the OBE and the CBE for services to football

Brian Clough

Brian Clough was born on the 21st March 1935

He played for Middlesbrough before a leg injury forced him to retire at 28

Brian Clough managed Leeds United for 44 days

He managed lowly Derby County with whom he won the League Championship in 1972

He managed Nottingham Forest for 18 years from 1975

Footynotes

Brian coined the phrases "young man" and "over the moon"

He played for England but not as many times as his son Nigel

He won two European Cups, the League Championship and four League Cups

He retired in 1993 when Nottingham Forest were relegated

Brian Clough was charged by the FA for illegal transfer payments

He hit a spectator and then kissed him to make it up with him

He is sadly missed in the game

Dixie Dean

Dixie Dean is remembered as the most prolific goalscorer in the history of English football

Dixie Dean was never booked or sent off in his long career

William Ralph "Dixie" Dean was born on 22nd January 1907 in Birkenhead

He died on March 1st 1980 at the age of 73 at his beloved Goodison Park watching a game between Everton and Liverpool

Dixie Dean scored 60 goals for Everton in the 1927-28 season at the age of 21

Dixie Dean began with Tranmere Rovers scoring 27 goals in 27 games in his first season

Dixie Dean joined Everton from Tranmere in 1925 for £3,000

Dixie Dean scored 32 goals in his first season with Everton

Dixie Dean scored 18 goals for England in 12 matches

Dixie Dean also played for Notts County towards the end of his career

Dixie Dean never won a single major honour in the game

Dixie Dean was 5' 10" tall

Dixie Dean fractured his skull in a motor bike accident in 1926

Dixie Dean hated his nickname; given due to his dark complexion and insisted he was called Bill

Dixie Dean scored 383 goals for Everton in 433 matches

Dixie Dean practiced heading with Tommy Lawton using a medicine ball

Dixie Dean scored a hat-trick for England against

Footynotes

Belgium in 1927 and another against Luxembourg 10 days later

Dixie Dean ended his career with Irish side Sligo Rovers

Dixie Dean ran a public house called the Dublin Packet in Chester after retiring

Dixie Dean also worked at Littlewoods Pools offices later in life where he worked as a porter

Pelé

Regarded by most as the World's greatest footballer of all time scoring 1280 goals in 1363 games

Born in Tras Coracoes, Brazil on 21st October 1940

Pelé's full name is Edson Arantes Do Nascimento

Pelé played for Santos at 15, Brazil at 16 and won the World Cup at 17

He earned money shining shoes at Baura Athletic Club

He was discovered by Medardo Olea

Pelé played for Brazilian clubs Santos and Noroeste as well as the New York Cosmos

Pelé played 92 times for Brazil and scored 77 goals

In a youth tournament in 1954 Pelé averaged almost 4 goals per game

Pelé claims Gordon Banks made the greatest ever save against him in the World Cup

Pelé played for Brazil shortly after his 16th birthday

He won FIFA's World Gold Medal for services to football in 1982

In 1966 he threatened to never play in the World Cup

again after constant fouls during games against Bulgaria and Portugal

His father played for Atletico Mineiro

Brazil never lost a match when Pelé and Garrincha were playing

He retired in 1977 as Brazil's greatest goalscorer of all time

His last international game was against Yugoslavia on July 18th 1971

Roy Of The Rovers

Roy Of The Rovers actual name was Roy Race

Roy Of The Rovers first appeared in *The Tiger* which was first published September 11th 1954

Roy Of The Rovers played for Melchester Rovers

Roy Of The Rovers was created by Frank S Pepper

Roy Of The Rovers played for 39 years until 1993 when he lost his foot in a helicopter crash

Roy Of The Rovers had a son Rocky who also played for Melchester

Roy Of The Rovers married his secretary Penny in 1976 and they had three children

Roy Of The Rovers played for England and managed them in a friendly against Holland

Melchester Rovers were founded in 1885

Roy Race and Blackie Gray both joined Melchester in 1954

Roy Of The Rovers scored 436 league goals

Blackie Gray's real name was William

Roy Of The Rovers' first kit was red and yellow shirt with blue shorts

Roy Of The Rovers became manager of Melchester Rovers on six different occasions

Roy Of The Rovers was signed by Ben Galloway

Roy Of The Rovers made a record with Gary Lineker in 1990

Roy Of The Rovers' grandfather Billy played for Melchester Rovers in the 1930s

Melchester Rovers won the league title 13 times

In 1989 Melchester Rovers moved to Wembley after an

...STEVE AND CHRIS KAMARA (*NOW SWINDON TOWN*) WERE PHOTOGRAPHED WITH ROY RACE!

earthquake at Mel Park

Roy Of The Rovers left Melchester Rovers in 1983 and signed for Walford Rovers but returned eight months later

Two members of pop group Spandau Ballet once played with Roy Of The Rovers at Melchester Rovers

Melchester Rovers was founded in 1885

Melchester Rovers became League Champions after 73 years of trying

Mel Park became Britain's first all seater stadium in 1983

Melchester Rovers' greatest win was 14-0 against Keysborough

Melchester Rovers appointed Roy Race as captain in 1958

Sir Alf Ramsey became caretaker manager of Melchester Rovers in 1982

Melchester Rovers changed from blue to red shorts in 1973

Melchester Rovers' away strip was blue shirts, white shorts and red socks which later changed to an all white strip

Melchester Rovers was purchased by Roy Race in 2001

In 1975 Melchester Rovers were knocked out of the cup by non-league Sleeford Town

The name Melchester Rovers has been used by other teams but legal action has never been taken

Melchester Rovers won the cup 11 times over 72 years

Melchester Rovers and its directors have not given an interview since 2000

Melchester Rovers were relegated in 1981

In 1986 Melchester Rovers went 12 league games

without conceding a goal

Melchester Rovers lost eight of its players to a terrorist attack in 1986

Football history

Britain's public schools played a major role in football development. Eton introduced goal nets and one of the first illustrations of football comes from Rugby School in 1863 showing pupils kicking a round ball. They picked up the ball and ran with it in 1923 and hello rugby. Up till that time it had been simply known as playground violence

The first televised football match was in 1936 between Arsenal and Everton

Footynote: And so began the illustrious TV career of Chris Kamara

The first Football League match played on a Sunday was Millwall v Fulham in 1974

Footynote; A nice quiet affair in a leafy suburb of London

White footballs became official on 9th November 1951 and were first used for floodlit matches

Footynote; Kammy was the first player to wear white boots, but only in the discos on a Saturday night

The 1878 FA Cup final was refereed by a Mr Bastard

Footynote; We reckon his Christian name was Useless

The Professional Footballers Association was formed on 2nd December 1907

Footynote; It came about because the Football League had finally ratified the maximum wage of £4 per week in 1901

Northern Ireland didn't play a foreign team until 1951 when they played France, even though they were founded in 1880 and are the fourth oldest international side

Footynote; Who did they play before that then? Their sisters' boyfriends?

Football is played in more countries than any other sport

Footynote; Most of whom now find it quite easy to draw 0-0 with England

Football was invented in China in 2500BC

Footynote; Prove us wrong, you weren't there

Football was originally called Tsu Chu

Footynote: As was the first Chinese international player. Prove us wrong again, you weren't there

Balls were made from animal skins until the ball as we now know it was developed in Mexico around 600AD

Footynote: The first ball may well have been made up from 500 shrews then?

In the early 19th Century some games were 200 a side

Footynote: The makers of Subbuteo probably put an end to that

Footynotes

Crossbars were introduced in 1875 replacing a piece of rope

Footynote; The rope caused problems in Liverpool when housewives hung out their washing on match days

Teams wearing different colour shirts were introduced in 1840

Footynote; Made Kammy's life easier…. Or you would think so

Corner kicks were introduced in 1872 and penalties in 1891

Footynote; As were mugs of Bovril at half time

In 1912 goalkeepers were banned from handling the ball outside the penalty area

Footynote; This stopped them stealing the ball at the end of the game and taking it home

The following year players had to be 10 yards from the ball at a free kick

Footynote; They started holding onto themselves the same year

Notts County are the world's oldest professional club and Sheffield are the oldest amateur club

Footynote; Kammy may have managed both of them. He can't think that far back

Preston North End beat Hyde 26-0 in a first round FA Cup match in 1887

Footynote; The 25th was a disputed affair with claims for offside

Shinpads were introduced in 1874 by Samuel Widdowson

Footynote: Vinnie Jones was born in Watford in 1965

Footynotes

The first floodlit match was in Sheffield in 1878

Footynote; Must have been at those Services on the M1

Numbers on shirts were enforced in 1939

Footynote; In 1939 someone said if you don't put numbers on shirts there will be a war

When the European Cup was founded in 1956 Real Madrid won it for five consecutive years

Footynote; In those borrowed shirts we mentioned earlier

The first British club to win the European Cup were Celtic in 1967 followed by Manchester United the following year
Footynote; We weren't actually in Europe then but who cares?

The Australian team was not founded until 1961
Footynote; They looked strange turning out wearing rubber hats and swimming shorts

Wendy Toms was the first female referee's assistant
Footynote; Ah yes, we all remember dear old Wendy

Footyclub trivia

Crystal Palace are the only club whose name begins with five consonants

Footynote; And who cares?

Chelsea were the last club to win at the old Wembley and the first to win at the new Wembley

Footynote; They just hung around there and saved Mr Abramovich some petrol money

Norwich reached third place in the Premiership in 1993

Footynote; Delia Smith baked a cake and decorated it with the message "come on let's be 'aving ya"

Leeds City were wound up in 1919 through financial dealings and returned the following year as Leeds United

Footynote; Something to do with Chris Kamara's hefty transfer fee

Blackburn Rovers are the earliest cup winners still in existence

Footynote; At least as we go to print

In 1933 Walsall beat the mighty Arsenal 2-0 in the cup

Footynote; No wonder they signed Theo Walcott

The first Wembley final was the 1923 FA Cup final between West Ham and Bolton Wanderers. It was nicknamed the white horse final after a police horse that kept back the pitch invaders

Footnote: What a job to be saddled with

Just so you know the policeman was PC George Scorey and the white horse was called Billie

Footnote: As in the song Billie don't be a hero

The 2003 Champions League final between AC Milan and Juventus was played at Old Trafford

Footnote: Yes, and the 2008 Champions League final between Manchester United and Chelsea was played in Moscow. So does this mean that Lokomotiv Moscow will play Zenit St Petersburg at Bernabeu next?

Arsenal wear red shirts in respect of Nottingham Forest who provided them with their first kit

Footynote: They also gave them Tony Woodcock and as a mark of respect they all played with big perms

Juventus play in black and white stripes the same as Notts County who gave them their first kit

Footynote: So if your club need a new kit get in touch with good old Notts County

Real Madrid play in all white to respect Old Corinthians although some say it was Swansea

Footynote: Either way, surely they could have found a plain white strip of their own?

Everton were a church side in 1878 but they left their ground, Anfield after a rent dispute and the landlord founded Liverpool

Footynote: On the seventh day was born little baby Rooney in a stable

AC Milan was founded in 1899 by English ex-pats as a football and cricket club

Footynote; And as we all know cricket really caught on in Italy

West Ham were originally the Thames Ironworkers, thus the nickname The Hammers

Footynote; Their hammers were put away until they unloaded Carlos Tevez

Benfica of Portugal were originally a cycling club

Footynote; So said their spokes-person

Celtic was founded in 1888 to raise funds for the poor children of Glasgow

Footnote: So in a credit crunch when you can't buy your kids presents get in touch with 'em!!

Colo Colo of Chile were the first South American club to play in Europe

Footnote: Isn't it a drink?

In 1963 playing Crystal Palace in a third round cup game Mansfield Town had 10 players booked

Footnote: So the ref had more numbers in his book than Sven Goran Eriksson

Sven Goran Eriksson has won the double in three different countries

Footnote: After three doubles Kammy can't remember a thing

Stamford Bridge was originally built for Fulham

Footnote: So presumably Craven Cottage was built for a small family called Craven?

No English manager has ever won the Premiership

Footynote: Don't hold your breath

There are 100 staircases at Arsenal's Emirates Stadium which would allow you to climb Canary Wharf twice

Footynote: So the fans are fitter than some of the visiting sides

The two clubs Dagenham and Redbridge merged in 1992

Footynote: So why didn't they call themselves Red Ham United?

Footynotes

Cardiff City are the only non-English club to win an FA Cup final

Footynote: Have you seen the Arsenal line-up lately?

The oldest Scottish club is Queens Park which was founded in 1867

Footynote: And the Scots invented golf so credit where it's due

Footyclub facts

Aston Villa

Two men called Matthews and one named Hughes
Three men who were about to break the news
These chapel goers would fulfil a dream
And become the first Aston Villa team
It all began a few years before
In the year of 1874

Down Heathfield Road the stories say
From Villa Cross Chapel they made their way
Walter Price their captain then
Summoned fifteen willing men
Fifteen players history books say
Played for Villa Cross Chapel on that day

Aston Brook St Mary's team
Thought they would win so it would seem
Everyone agreed until

Kammy and Digance

Aston Villa won 1-0
The first half was to rugby's rule
But in the second half they changed the ball

Jack Hughes goal proved to be the killer
The first to score for Aston Villa
George Ramsey was a Scottish chap
Who always wore a polo cap
The first of Villa's greatest names
As they rose to fame through their early games

Then they moved to Perry Barr
A better ground and not so far
The first home gate was 5s 3d
In modern money 28p
April 1887
Aston Villa were in heaven

At last they won the FA Cup
West Bromwich were the runners-up
In the 1890s they made their mark
And set up home at Villa Park
Johnny Campbell another Scot
The first goal at Villa Park he got

Footynotes

Kammy and Digance

By 1910 they reigned supreme
Forever onward strode the team
35 years since that congregation
found Aston Villa their salvation
A player of whom all would talk
Peter McParland from Dundalk

An exciting player at number 11
Won the cup in 1957
Dixon, Aldis, Crowther, Pace, Birch, Lynn
Myercough, Seweel, Mith and Sims
The players of 1957
When the FA Cup was raised to heaven

Ray Wood, broken jaw
United keeper on the floor
Jackie Blanchflower, remember that?
The only half back to wear a hat
Now the early Villa story is told
Some have died, some are old

Heathfield Road is sadly gone
But Aston Villa marches on
Walking home from church that day

It seems so many years away
Who would have thought that congregation
Would build one of the best teams of the nation?

Coming up......

Arsenal
Barcelona
Chelsea
Liverpool
Manchester United
Notts County
Real Madrid

Arsenal

Arsenal wear red shirts in respect of Nottingham Forest who gave them their first kit as we've already mentioned but what happens if Nottingham Forest suddenly start wearing blue?

Arsenal were founded in 1886 by ammunition workers

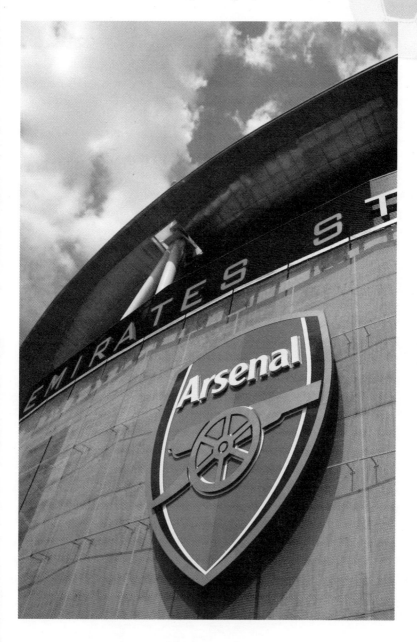

at the Royal Arsenal in Woolwich, South London

The Arsenal's workers provided weapons for the Crimean War

The club was originally known as Dial Square after one of the workshops

The club became Woolwich Arsenal in 1891

That's why they're known as The Gunners

They started out on the other side of London to where they are now

They were The Arsenal until 1927 when they changed their name to Arsenal

Arsenal were relegated in 1913 after winning just one game all season

Their first game was against Eastern Wanderers in 1886

Herbert Chapman became their manager in 1925 and the success story began

Chapman signed Alex James and Cliff Bastin two Arsenal legends

Billy Wright, Wolves and England captain, became manager in 1961

Arsenal were promoted to the First Division in 1904

The first Arsenal international player was Caesar Jenkins who played for Wales in 1896

Goalkeeper David Seaman played 563 games

England 1966 hero the late Alan Ball joined Arsenal from Everton

David O'Leary played 722 games between 1975 and 1993

Thierry Henry played 357 games and scored 221 goals before joining Barcelona

Patrick Vieira played 79 times for France whilst at Arsenal

Emmanuel Petit of France was the first Arsenal player to play in a World Cup final

In 1970 -71 Arsenal won 29 of their 42 games

Their first game at Highbury was against Leicester in 1913

When striker John Radford joined West Ham he played 91 games and did not score a goal

Captain Tony Adams served a prison sentence for a driving offence

David Rocastle, an Arsenal favourite, sadly died of cancer in 2001 aged just 33

Their first game at the new Emirates Stadium was against Ajax of Holland, July 22nd 2006

Arsenal won the European Cup Winners Cup in 1994

beating Parma 1-0

They won the league and cup double in 1971 and again in 1997-98

Arsene Wenger was the first foreign manager ever to win the Championship

Barcelona

"Catalonia is a country and Barcelona is their army"
Sir Bobby Robson 1996

Barcelona's story begins on 22nd October 1899 when Joan Gampers placed an ad in the *Los Deportes* newspapers seeking players

The first club meeting took place and consisted of Swiss, English and Catalan responders to the ad

Real Madrid and Athletic Bilbao also have English founders

Footynotes

Barcelona were founded in 1899

Barcelona's club motto is "more than a club"

Barcelona fans are known as culers

Barcelona were the first La Liga Champions in 1928

In 2005-2006 Barcelona's revenue was £259 million, making them the second richest club in the world

Barcelona won their first Cup final in 1902

Paulino Alcantara scored 356 goals for Barcelona

In 1961 Barcelona were the first club to beat Real Madrid in a European Cup match

The Camp Nou Stadium was completed in 1957

Johan Cruyff joined Barcelona from Ajax in 1973 and became manager in 1988

Cruyff chose Barcelona over Real Madrid as he refused

to play for a club under Franco

Johan Cruyff's son Jordi, ex Manchester United, has a Catalan name

Terry Venables became manager in 1984

Gary Lineker joined Barcelona after the 1986 World Cup finals

Chelsea

Chelsea football ground is not in Chelsea but in Fulham

Chelsea was founded in 1905

Their old stand sported a weather vane depicting a model of striker George Hilsdon

Ted Drake became manager in 1915

Roman Abramovich bought Chelsea in 2003 for £140m

Chelsea have never moved grounds since they were founded

Tommy Docherty changed the colour of their shorts to blue when he was manager

Chelsea's first shirt sponsors were Gulf Air

Ron Harris played 795 games

Chelsea were the first club to fly to a league game in 1957 when they flew to Newcastle

Chelsea were the first club to wear numbered shirts in 1928

The first English club to field a totally non-English side in 2007 against Southampton

Kerry Dixon was signed from Reading and scored 193 goals

Jimmy Greaves scored 41 goals in the 1961-62 season

Frank Lampard and Ray Wilkins are the only players to win consecutive Player of the Year awards

Chelsea won the league for the first time in 1954

In 1966 Chelsea wore an Inter Milan strip against Sheffield Wednesday

Jack Harrow from 1911 was the first player to make 300 appearances for Chelsea

Willi Steffan of Switzerland became Chelsea's first foreign player in 1946

Allan Harris was the first player to leave and rejoin Chelsea

In the first game at Stamford Bridge they beat Liverpool 4-0

David Calderhead managed Chelsea for 26 years

George Mills was the first Chelsea player to score 100 goals

Roy Bentley was signed from Newcastle for £11,500

Jimmy Greaves was sold to AC Milan in 1961

Jimmy Greaves scored 122 goals in just four seasons

In 1953 Chelsea were beaten 8-1 by Wolves

Blue Is The Colour reached number five in the pop charts

Geoff Hurst became manager in 1979

Gus and Joseph Mears purchased Stamford Bridge Athletic Ground in 1896

Chelsea lost their first league game to Stockport County in 1905

John Robertson was the club's first player-manager

Chelsea goalkeeper Willie Foulke weighed 22 stone

Liverpool

Liverpool were founded in 1892 by John Houlding after Everton vacated the Anfield ground

Liverpool originally played in blue and white

The Kop was named after a hill in Natal where a battle took place during the Boer War

Liverpool's first ever game was against Higher Walton which they won 8-0

Liverpool were elected to the Football League in 1893

They won their first League Championship in 1901

John McKenna was the club's first non-English manager

You'll Never Walk Alone was written by Rogers and Hammerstein for the musical Carousel but is associated with Gerry and the Pacemakers

You'll Never Walk Alone adorns the Shankly Gates which

Footynotes

were opened in 1982

In 1914 they were beaten 1-0 by Burnley in their first FA Cup final

In 1954 Liverpool were beaten 9-1 by Birmingham

Bill Shankly became manager of Liverpool in 1959 after being a player with Huddersfield Town

In his first season as manager he released 24 players

Liverpool won the FA Cup for the first time in 1965, beating Leeds

Liverpool won the UEFA Cup in 1971

Bill Shankly retired as manager in 1974, replaced by fellow Scot Bob Paisley

In 1983 under Joe Fagan Liverpool were the first English club to win three major trophies

In 1985 Liverpool reached the European Cup final

when they were beaten by Juventus at the Heysel Stadium where the sad disaster took place

Liverpool legend Kenny Dalglish was the club's first player-manager in 1985

Ephraim Longworth was the first Liverpool player to captain England in 1921

Nearly 100 Liverpool fans sadly died at Hillsborough during a game between Liverpool and Nottingham Forest on 15th April 1989

George Gillett and Tom Hicks took ownership of Liverpool in 2007

Bob Paisley signed Alan Hansen, Kenny Dalglish and Ian Rush

Liverpool played in all red for the first time in 1964 under Bill Shankly

Liverpool have won the league title 18 times

Ian Rush scored 346 goals for Liverpool

Robbie Fowler scored a hat-trick against Arsenal in just four minutes and 32 seconds in the 1994-95 season

Steven Gerrard is Liverpool's leading goalscorer in European competitions

Manchester United

Manchester United were the first team to win the double three times in 1994, 1996 and 1999

Paul Ince when at Manchester United became the first black captain of England

Mark Hughes scored United's first ever Premiership goal against Sheffield United in 1992

They were originally called Newton Heath Cricket and Football Club and were founded in 1878

Newton Heath went bankrupt in 1902

They first won the Manchester Cup in 1886

Manchester United had seven players in the England side against Albania in 2001, though two were subs

Billy Meredith always played with a tooth-pick in the side of his mouth for good luck

Eric Cantona has been voted Manchester United's greatest player of all time

They won the league for the first time in 1908

George Best played 466 times and scored 178 goals

When Duncan Edwards died in the Munich air disaster he was only 21 but had already played for England 18 times

Newton Heath's first ground was at North Road, Monsall

Manchester United played their first game at Old

Trafford in 1910 against Liverpool

Their first game after the Munich air disaster was against Sheffield Wednesday

Sir Matt Busby didn't buy any players between 1953 and 1957

In the 1951-52 season Jack Rowley scored three hat-tricks in 22 days

George Best was United's leading scorer in five successive seasons

Bobby Charlton made his debut in 1956 against Charlton and scored twice

Martin Buchan captained both an FA Cup and Scottish Cup winning side

From 1964-72 Manchester United bought only three players. Ian Ure, Alex Stepney and Willie Morgan

Manchester United have twice had brothers appear in

an FA Cup final. Gary and Phil Neville and Brian and Jimmy Greenhoff

Sir Matt Busby played once for Scotland

Bobby Charlton played 752 times and scored 247 goals

Ryan Giggs scored Manchester United's quickest ever goal, 15 seconds against Southampton in 1995

In 1905 Charlie Roberts was the first Manchester United player to play for England

Eric Cantona took 19 penalties for Manchester United and scored 17 times

Eric Cantona played 45 times for France

David Beckham turned up for a trial with Tottenham Hotspur wearing a Manchester United shirt

Sir Matt Busby was appointed manager of Scotland in 1958

In his debut against Portsmouth in 1987 Steve Bruce gave away a penalty, was booked and busted his nose

Notts County

Here we pay tribute to Notts County the oldest professional football club in the world

One of the clubs in the original Football League in 1888

No club has moved divisions more than Notts County. They have been relegated 14 times and promoted 15 times

Notts County moved to Meadow Lane in 1910

Juventus played in pink shirts with polka dots until John Savage sorted them out with black and white striped shirts from Notts County in 1903

Notable Notts County players; Tommy Lawton, Dixie

Kammy and Digance

Dean, Jermaine Pennant, Tony Hateley, Jeff Astle, Jackie Sewell, Steve Finnan, Craig Short, Dave Watson, Geoff Pike, John Chidozie

Sam Allardyce, once managed Notts County before moving to Bolton

Neil Warnock managed Notts County until 1993

Their club song "County's The Team For Me" was voted the worst song of all time by Noel Edmonds

Notts County is three years older than rivals Nottingham Forest

In 1872 Notts County played in black and yellow hoops

In 1894 Notts County won the FA Cup for the one and only time

They were the first Second Division club to win the FA Cup after being relegated

England legend Tommy Lawton joined Notts County in

1946, a bit like Cristiano Ronaldo joining them today

Notts County became known as the Magpies because of their black and white stripes although after World War Two they played in white shirts

Notts County beat Newport in 1949 11-1

Notts County beat Rotherham 15-1 in the FA Cup in 1885

Goalkeeper Albert Iremonger played 564 games from 1904

Real Madrid

Real Madrid built the first multi-national side in the 1950s

Real Madrid was founded on March 6th 1902, their original name was Madrid

Before Real Madrid there was another club Football Sky which was founded by English students amongst others

Footynotes

and it split into two

Real being Spanish for royal was added in 1920, granted by King Alfonso XIII

Real Madrid's former coach after World War Two was Don Santiago Bernabeu who they named their 110,000 seater stadium after. The stadium now holds 80,400 due to safety regulations

Real Madrid won the first European Cup in 1956 with players such as Puskas, di Stefano and Santamaria

Real Madrid have a purple band in their badge that represents the Kingdom of Castile

Real Madrid have won 30 league titles and won the European Cup eight times

Real Madrid signed David Beckham from Manchester United, negotiating their transfer fee on merchandise revenue

Real Madrid beat Eintrecht of Frankfurt 7-3 in the 1960

European Cup. Ferenc Puskas scored four goals and Alfredo di Stefano scored three

The game was played at Hampden Park and the attendance was 138,000

Real Madrid lured Fabio Capello from AC Milan in 1997. He was sacked on June 28th 2007 after the departure of David Beckham

Real Madrid manager Jupp Heynckes led Real Madrid to their seventh European Cup success and was sacked

Real Madrid signed England winger Laurie Cunningham who was killed in a car crash in Spain, other English signings were Steve McManaman and Michael Owen from Liverpool and Thomas Gravesen from Everton

Footygrams – clubs

Mix up the letters to find hidden football clubs. If you can't get the first couple then best you move on

Ham stew – **West Ham**

Underlands – **Sunderland** (we only moved one letter for heaven's sake)

Over net – **Everton**

Mouth strop – **Portsmouth**

Married lad – **Real Madrid**

My bowstring – **Grimsby Town**

Tee strained munch – **Manchester United**

A lost anvil – **Aston Villa**

Rely nub – **Burnley**

Acute swindle ten – **Newcastle United**

A shot-putter month – **Tottenham Hotspur**

Toy kites c – **Stoke City**

Law teaching IT – **Wigan Athletic**

Try nee lotion – **Leyton Orient**

Seal ran – **Arsenal**

Er Romans revert – **Tranmere Rovers**

Oil over LP – **Liverpool**

England

Charles William Alcock is a name few people know.
Which is really quite surprising, as far as important
people go.
Years ago Charles Alcock had a very special dream.
He set about the forming of the England Football team.
November 1870, The Glasgow Herald ran a letter
Saying "England will play Scotland and the more who
came the better."

Charles William Alcock was referee; to keep an eye on
who turned up.
He founded the FA, and then invented the FA Cup.
Wanderers were the first cup winners
And again he did 'em like a kipper.
Cos when Wanderers won the cup….guess what?
Alcock was their skipper.

He thought England playing Scotland would be a
tasty menu.
He also thought the Oval would be a tasty venue.

Footynotes

Kammy and Digance

How would he book the cricket ground?
For him there was no worry.
Why? Charles William Alcock also played for Surrey.

The Olympic Games in London, the year 1908.
Something else Charles William Alcock would help
to instigate.
Football could be included,
It just needed someone to suggest it.
Who came up with the idea?
Of course he did, you've guessed it!

Denmark started favourites but England won two nought.
And became Olympic champions, the first ever, in this
sport.
Charles William Alcock, our busiest ever so and so
And that's why I wrote this poem, I thought you should
know.

In 1953 Hungary became the first country to beat England at Wembley

Footynote: But sadly more followed

England are the only country to win the World

Footynotes

Cup playing in red
Footynote: Only because Bristol City don't qualify

Teddy Sheringham was an England substitute 21 times
Footynote: But he played more times for England than Geoff Hurst

Ian Wright played just nine full games for England but he was a substitute 16 times
Footynote: Now there's a gladiator for you

Arsenal captain Tony Adams played 421 games for Arsenal but didn't captain England until he was 28

Footnote: Tony's nickname was Rodders after the Nicholas Lyndhurst character in *Only Fools and Horses.* I don't believe it Kammy

Billy Foulke was the heaviest man to play for England at 22 stone

Footnote: Further confirmation that Kammy didn't play for England

Alan Mullery was the first to be sent off playing for England

Footnote: Even further confirmation Kammy didn't play for England

Alan Mullery pulled out of England's games in 1964 because he wrenched his back cleaning his teeth

Footnote: Why did he have to bend down to reach his teeth then?

Alan Shearer was England's 100th captain

Footynote; Proving it can never have a job description including the word secure

Neil Webb of Nottingham Forest was England's 1,000th player

Footynote; He replaced Glenn Hoddle

Arthur Milton of Arsenal played cricket and football for England

Footynote; Pelé didn't

Cricketer Leslie Compton played football for England against Wales at the age of 38. The oldest England player

Footynote; Never overlook that Chris Kamara. It's never too late

At 18 years and 236 days Wayne Rooney became the youngest England player

Footynote; Kammy can't really beat that now to be honest

In 1890 England played two internationals in the same day, against Wales and Ireland

Footynote; Must have been a petrol shortage

In 1934 against Italy England fielded seven Arsenal players

Footynote: Not much chance of that today

Bobby Charlton scored his 100th goal for England at Wembley against Northern Ireland and he scored

Footynote: It could have been Ralph Coates, they looked similar from a distance

The lowest crowd to ever watch an England match at Wembley was 15,628 against Chile in 1989

Footynote: And they're still claiming ticket refunds to this day

The first all-seated international that sold out at Wembley was against Brazil in 1990

Footynote: Meaning the crowd of course and not the players

In a match between England and Malta in 1971 goalkeeper Gordon Banks didn't touch the ball

Footynote: He didn't want to get involved

Kammy and Digance

Footynotes

Although Billy Wright played over 100 times for England he'd only played 50 of them by the age of 30

Footynote; Kammy has worked out the rest were played after he was 30

England international Stan Mortensen of Blackpool played for Wales against England in 1943

Footynote; Confused dot com

Bobby Moore and Billy Wright both captained England 90 times

Footynote; 90 more times than someone we know

1966 England hero Ray Wilson became an undertaker when he retired from football

Footynote; Yeah, we just had to dig that one up

England have played Brazil 22 times and won just four

Footynote; So Brazil have fielded four dodgy teams in their time then

Footynotes

Players who played in the 1966 World Cup finals for England but never made the final were Terry Paine, Jimmy Greaves, Ian Callaghan and John Connelly

Footynote: Like the ball perhaps they never crossed the line

The 1966 winning team played together unchanged until April 1967 when Roger Hunt was replaced by Jimmy Greaves

Footynote: Jimmy Greaves says he doesn't remember this. Indeed Jimmy Greaves says he doesn't remember the 1960s

Sven Goran Eriksson was the first football manager to substitute the entire team at half time against Holland in 2001

Footynote: If people in Poland are called Poles why aren't people in Holland called Holes?

England played their first international in 1872 against Scotland in Glasgow. It ended nil-nil

Footynote: It was the same score at half time

Terry Venables was the only player to represent England at every single level from schoolboy onwards and then became coach and England's most successful manager losing only two games out of 23

Footynote: He also claimed to be a pop singer, as did Chris Waddle and Glenn Hoddle

Footynotes

In 1876 three brothers played for England; Arthur, Edward and Ernest Bambridge

Footynote: In some England sides their mum would have got a game too

Norman Bailey of Corinthians was the first English international player to reach double figures of appearances. Of his 19 games 10 were against Scotland

Footynote: Which goes to prove that Hadrian's Wall wasn't high enough

William Slaney who was born in India was the first England player born overseas

Footynote: Did he win an England cap or a turban?

Viv Anderson was the first black England player

Footynote: So close Kammy

England played their first indoor international against Argentina in 2002

Footynote: It made it easier to hear the tackles go in

Jimmy Mullen of Wolves became England's first ever substitute in 1950 when he replaced Newcastle's Jackie Milburn

Footynote: We reckon that went down really well in Newcastle

The famous World War One game between England and Germany took place on Christmas Day 1914 when fighting ceased and the game was played. Fighting continued the following day

Footynote: Kammy was born on Christmas Day but there was no sign of three wise men

The World Cup

Do you ever think the World Cup is a fix
England won it in 1966
And on that year of celebration
They just so happened to be the home nation
1930 was the year of the World Cup's inauguration
Uruguay won the first World Cup they too being the
host nation
Italy hosted in 1934
And the host nation won the World Cup once more
So here's a plan if all else fails
Make sure the next one takes place in Wales

Scotland were eliminated from the World Cup in 1974 without losing a game
Footynote: How did they not win it - Kenny Dalglish, Billy Bremner, Denis Law, Lorimer, McGrain and Johnstone?

Uruguay won the first World Cup in 1930
Footynote: Fair enough it was their ball and their garden. Similar thing happened in 1966

In the 1994 World Cup Bulgaria were the only team ever fielded in which all 11 names ended in OV

Footynote; And when they were knocked out that's exactly what they did

When Uruguay won the World Cup in 1930 they had a player Hector Castro who didn't have a left hand

Footynote; We presume he left the lifting of the trophy to someone else

Wales though founded in 1876 didn't reach the World Cup finals until 1958

Footynote; But with a different team to that in 1876 perhaps?

Scotland were playing Estonia in a World Cup qualifying game in 1996. Due to a dispute over floodlights Estonia didn't show up. Scotland kicked off and the final whistle was immediately blown

Footynote; So who won?

Italy were the first European country to win the World Cup

Footynote: Four years later they surrendered…their world title

India once withdrew from the World Cup because they weren't allowed to play in bare feet

Footynote: Delete from the above fact "in bare feet" and you're closer to the truth

Switzerland fielded a side in 1966 that included players Eichmann and Fuhrer

Footynote; And the crowd sang "you'll never yodel alone"

The highest number of yellow cards in a World Cup finals game is 16. On two occasions; Germany v Cameroon in 2002 and Portugal v Holland in 2006

Footynote; The British countries haven't picked up too many for obvious reasons

The World Cup was hidden under the bed of a prominent Italian politician in World War Two to keep it safe from the Nazis

Footynote; They planned to melt it down and convert it into a Messerschmitt

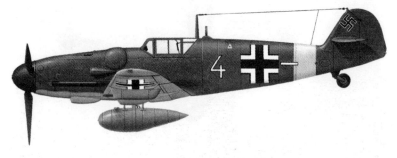

Footynotes

The USA beat England 1-0 in the 1950 World Cup finals with a goal from Larry Gaetjens. The England team included Tom Finney and Stan Mortensen

Footynote: So that amazing fact is possibly what lured Beckham to the USA

In the 1998 finals in France, Iran beat the United States

Footynote: Watch this space because revenge could be on the cards

Tunisia was the first African side to win a World Cup finals match when they beat Mexico in 1978

Footnote; But they did use a special kind of grass

Colombian Andres Escobar was shot dead after scoring an own goal in 1994

Footnote; Who was that Liverpool full back who did a runner at the end of the 2007-08 season?

In the 1930 game between Mexico and Argentina referee Ulrico Saucedo awarded five penalties

Footnote; He was never found

In 1990 Costa Rica finished second in their group having employed five different managers since qualifying

Footnote; So there's still hope for Leicester City

Brazil are the only country to have appeared in the final stages of every World Cup

Footnote; If only their players had Welsh grandparents

Roger Milla of The Cameroons is the oldest World Cup outfield player at 42 years and 39 days

Footynote; Some say he could have been older!

In the 1986 finals in Mexico Jose Batista of Uruguay was sent off against Scotland after just 54 seconds

Footynote; Just a minute….oh yes just a minute

In the 1956 World Cup at Goodison Park Eusebio scored four of Portugal's five goals when they beat North Korea 5-3

Footynote; Why isn't there a West and East Korea then?

In the 1994 finals Russia's Oleg Salenko scored five goals against Cameroon

Footynote; He'd be a Chelsea player today we reckon

Footynotes

Footygrams – grounds

More Footygrams to unravel. Try and find the names of these hidden football grounds. As always we start with a few easy ones just in case you want to try working them out with your granny

Smartys – **St Mary's**

Deepened – **Deep Dene**

Mark Hope – **Home Park**

Find ale – **Anfield**

Near a choir – **Ricoh Arena**

Allan Marble – **Bramall Lane**

Rapid Perk – **Pride Park**

Unbelievable facts

John Ritchie of Stoke City and John McAlle of Wolves have both been sent off without kicking a ball

Footynote; Kammy was once sent off for not kicking a ball after 89 minutes

The quickest ever throw-in after the start of a game is three seconds when Paul Kitson of West Ham kicked the ball into touch from the kick-off

Footynote; We seem to remember this day. The bookies had a bad day which of course had nothing whatsoever to do with the above incident

Bobby Collins of Everton wore size four boots

Footynote; So did Kanu but he was only six months old at the time

In January 1983 Weymouth players went on strike before a game against Maidstone over

travelling arrangements. They were docked 10 league points

Footynote; We seem to remember Eric Cantona had a similar travel problem involving a fishing trawler and a bunch of seagulls

There was once a movie called *The Arsenal Stadium Mystery* from the book of the same name by Leonard Gribble

Footynote; Is that why their former stadium used to be called "Library"?

In a football match between Sheffield Wednesday and Sheffield United referee Walter Brennan, a schoolteacher, officiated over three of his former pupils

Footynote: So its possible he gave them detentions as opposed to yellow cards

In 1977 Joe Craig of Scotland scored in his very first international with his very first touch

Footynote: Jose Mourinho would have substituted for not sticking to the game plan

On 31st August 1984 the longest football match started. It lasted 68 hours and 11 minutes and was between two sides in Palm Beach, Florida

Footynote: The game between Croatia and Turkey at Euro 2008 seemed to last longer though

Footynotes

Footyrhymes

The Jungle Cup Final

On Saturday, weather permitting, of course,
The Jungle Cup final takes place.
The Giraffes play Gorilla Athletic,
A rough bunch and a hard team to face.

The Gorillas know nothing of tactics or ploy,
They grab hold of the ball and they run.
They've played twenty-eight
games since
the monsoon last year
And so far they haven't
lost one.

The Giraffes, on the other hand, count on their skills,
A sort of long-necked Brazil.
They're sticking those necks out and saying they'll win,
But few think they actually will.

Their road to the final was merely a stroll,
In the first round they knocked out the Snails.
They had a second-round bye against Scorpion Town,
Who kept bursting the ball with their tails.

Footynotes

Kammy and Digance

In the third round they knocked out the Python eleven,
The Giraffes being fast and quite tall.
They played for an hour and ten minutes or more,
And only one Python headed the ball.

It was the high balls into the centre
The Pythons just could not match.
But hugging each other after the game
The Pythons broke two Giraffes' backs.

Kammy and Digance

The second round Lemming match, that was a farce.
The goalkeeper climbed up the post,
Then jumped off as soon as Gorillas attacked
And if he hadn't, it would have been close.

So that's how they made the grand final today.
It's five minutes gone with no score.
A Gorilla's already been sent off for chewing
And by full time there could be some more.

Giraffes are attacking, it's two against two,
Now Greg, their best player, is through.

Athletic close in and break all his legs
And the Gorillas sent off moves to two.

"Penalty," yells the capacity crowd
And Giraffes score a goal from
the spot.
One more Gorilla goes off
for dissent,
For he swore black
and blue it
was not.

Footynotes

Kammy and Digance

Come half time Gorillas were down to eight men
And not looking terribly pleased.
The Giraffes suck some lemons and sponge
down their necks
While Athletic chew up a few trees.

The referee blows and the second half starts
And Giraffes get a goal from the start.
Two goals behind and three lads sent off,
The Gorillas begin to lose heart.

"Easy, easy," the spectators cry,
As Johnny Giraffe gets a goal.
A Gorilla disputes that Giraffes
were offside
And swallows the
referee whole.

The Elephant riot
squad run on to
the pitch
To hold back the
menacing crowd,
Who were rather upset by

Athletics' approach,
For eating the ref's, not allowed.

The match was abandoned, Giraffes won the cup,
Much to Athletics' dismay.
On the way home it was agreed that Giraffes
Were the far better team on the day.

The Jungle Cup Final Return

Every year when the Jungle Cup final takes place,
There's no Liverpools, nor Aston Villas.
There are graceful teams like Giraffes and Swans
And dirty teams like the Gorillas.

In the previous year, Giraffes took the cup,
Much to Gorillas surprise.
The Giraffes and Gorillas were meeting again,
Having won all their previous ties.

Giraffes had knocked out the Elephants
And had no problem beating the Voles.
They expectedly hammered the Spiders
(And in the process scored thirty-nine goals)

But the Spiders did well to get where they did,
With a shock win against the Partridges.
Due to weak legs most stayed in their webs
With damaged knee-cap and cartilages.

Giraffes really played Spiders' reserves,
And the thrashing was hardly surprising.

Kammy and Digance

Eleven brave chaps played 'til they collapsed
And their injury list kept on rising.

Gorillas dirty as usual,
Determined to take home the cup.
The first round Foxes left the ground in boxes
And the Ladybirds didn't turn up.

Their non-appearance was due, so they say,
To a strong lack of self-control.
They threatened to beat up Gorillas
If the furry beasts scored the first goal.

So they decided not to turn up at all.
Though a good excuse had to be made.
They said their houses were
burning down
And they awaited the fire brigade.

So the final kicked off, like
the year before,
With Gorillas on the
attack.
A Gorilla bit off a poor

Footynotes

Kammy and Digance

Giraffes head
And was booed for not giving it back.
"Although I'm headless I'll carry on,"
said the most courageous Giraffe.

He looked in great pain as again and again,
He headed the ball with his scarf.

"That's it, I just can't stand any more,"
As he walked from the field with regret.
Then the ball hit the lad on the back of
the neck
And ricocheted into the net.

The crowd went completely
bananas,
The Gorillas, one down
and so soon,
Were sick as
proverbial Parrots.
(Giraffes were
over the moon).

Ten minutes gone and a corner

Kammy and Digance

And Giraffes once again went so close.
But what a fine save by the keeper so brave,
Who then ate half the crossbar post.

Then just on the stroke of half time,
Johnny Giraffe scored another,
Gorillas demanded it be disallowed,
Or they'd eat up the referee's brother.

"I'm not open to bribes, the goal stands,"
Said the overworked ref tired and torrid.
Besides, he felt that was no big deal,
(He thought his brother was horrid).

Footynotes

Kammy and Digance

It looked like Giraffes would take home the cup,
So convincing its stature and style.
Yet Gorillas were finding their rhythm,
(So they sang and danced for a while).

Giraffes were getting too big for their boots,
Which explained their terrible blisters.
Most wore the cheapest boots money could buy.
(Tarquin Giraffe wore his sister's).

Yes, the ruffians were getting back in the game,
And forcing Giraffes to play deeper.
They not only pulled two goals back,
But also the arms of the keeper.

Footynotes

Kammy and Digance

Two goals and a few names into the book,
And the ref was playing it firm.
One Gorilla claimed to be Keegan,
Back-combing his fur like a perm.

As full time blew, the excitement grew,
They played extra time for the winner.
Giraffes' centre half had been nibbled all game.
And he looked considerably thinner.

He dribbled down the left side of the field,
Due to his lack of front teeth.

He crossed the ball to his team-mates so tall,
Yes, he certainly gave it some beef.

Over it came like a rocket,
The defence and attackers jumped up.
The ball found the head of right winger Jed,
And Giraffes, once again, won the cup.

Giraffes claimed to be invincible,
Though Gorillas' boss had his doubts.
He said he thought at the end of the day,

Footynotes

Kammy and Digance

They were there or thereabouts.

"It's application and attitude,
And whoever scored the most goals.
On the day it wasn't quite right,
I doubt if we'd beaten the Voles."

"I've said it before and I'll say it again,
The next game is always the toughest."
Giraffes simply said of all the teams they'd met,
Gorillas were by far the roughest.

Footynotes

Football Discipline

In the days before iPods and mobile phones
We'd never heard of metatarsal bones
Each late tackler when he makes 'em
Knows there's a chance that he's gonna break 'em
A particular foul springs to mind
That's when you get clobbered from behind
That's why a professional foul is its name
You can put another professional out of the game

You get taken off if the boss thinks you're skiving
But you get off quicker if you're seen to be diving
If you take off your shirt and wave it around
In the referee's pocket a yellow card will be found
Just so that you can show off your tattoos
A yellow card isn't brilliant news
So if you want to take off your shirt…do not
No matter what a great body you think you have got
For a foul you can pay the price really quick
Specially if Ronaldo takes the free kick

Nine Letter Football Teams

For us who love our football
Here is a little game
How many clubs in England and Scotland
Have nine letters in their name?

So far this is approximate
But give or take some tricks
In England there are seventeen
And in Scotland only six

Blackpool Blackburn start our ditty
Followed by Brentford Stockport and Leicester City
Tottenham, Cambridge and then here's a killer
We can cheat and include Aston Villa

Newcastle, Liverpool, Mansfield Town
And this is how you trick 'em
We can add the Wanderers, Bolton
Wolverhampton and the third is Wycombe

And if we should adopt a club
And have our name upon their sweaters

Kammy and Digance

It must be Sheffield Wednesday
Two words both of nine letters

And so we move to Scotland
With Clydebank we make a start on
Hibernian, Stranraer
and I've also found Dumbarton

If you know any others
Then your selections are invited
But for those of you in Scotland
You can't have Ayr United

Back Street International

I was very honoured when they named Wolves and
England legend Steve Bull after this poem. Bully used
the rhyme in his autobiography and I was delighted to
allow such a loyal one-club player to call himself the
back street international

I'm just eleven but I ain't stupid
My feet are firm on the ground
I was born on the wrong side of the city
To see the sun shining down
But at least I have my dreams
And some people don't know what that means
So don't pity my bashed about shoes
I can be anyone that I choose

I'm an international
And that's all I want to be
I'm an international
And that's good enough for me
I'm a back street international

Footyquiz

Who played for England whilst playing for Glasgow Rangers?

Answer: Paul Gascoigne in 1995

A number of British clubs names start and end with the same letter;

Answers: Liverpool, Celtic, Aston Villa, York City, Alloa, Dundee United, Charlton Athletic, Kilmarnock. Any more?

Three England captains who played for Scunthorpe;

Answers: Kevin Keegan, Ray Clemence and Ian Botham

The various second words of English football clubs;

United, Rangers, Wanderers, City, Palace, Hotspur, Villa,

Rovers, Alexandra, Vale, Argyle, Albion, County, Forest, Wednesday, Dons, Athletic, Orient, Town

An England team of four letter named players;

Wood, Neal, Cole A, Ball, Bell, Ince, Hill, Hunt, Owen, Cole J, Pegg

England side made up of past and present Manchester United players;

Stepney, Byrne, Neville, Styles, Edwards, Ferdinand, Rooney, Charlton, Smith, Violet, Connolly

England side made up of past and present West Ham United players;

James, Konchesky, Lampard Snr, Moore, Martin, Peters, Ferdinand, Cole J, Lampard, Hurst, Carrick

England side made up of past and present Arsenal players;

Seaman, Dixon, Cole A, Ball, Adams, Williams, Walcott, MacDonald, Radford, Kennedy, Lawton

England side made up of past and present Tottenham Hotspur players;

Robinson, Ramsey, Mullery, Carrick, Campbell, Gascoigne, Lennon, Greaves, Smith, Allen, Peters

England side made up of past and present Liverpool players;

Clemence, Neal, Lawler, Hughes, Carragher, Thompson, Redknapp, Gerrard, Owen, Hunt, Crouch

England side made up past and present Blackburn Rovers players;

Flowers, Crompton, Le Saux, Clayton, Blackburn, Batty, Ripley, Bentley, Douglas, Shearer, Campbell

Kammy and Digance

Footynotes

Scotland side made up of Football Managers;

Brown, Burley, McNeill, Graham, Ferguson, Souness, Strachan, Dalglish, Sturrock, McCoist, Robertson

Terry Curran played for 14 different Football League clubs. Can you name them?

Answer: No

Three England players with three 'O's' in their surnames;

Answer: Peter Osgood, Tony Woodcock and Ian Storey-Moore

Great English players who never played for England;

Billy Bonds (West Ham), Ted Phillips (Ipswich Town), Mike Marsh, (Liverpool), Chris Turner (Sunderland), Chris Kamara (various)

Great English players who played for England just once;

David Pegg (Manchester United), Phil Parkes (West Ham), Tommy Smith (Liverpool), Ron Henry (Tottenham), Nigel Jemson (Nottingham Forest), John Fantham

(Sheffield Wednesday), Mick Phelan (Manchester United), Danny Clapton (Arsenal), Jim Cutliffe (Everton), George Eastham (Blackpool)

Eleven England players with strange hair-styles;

Seaman, Bobby Charlton, Waddle, Hoddle, Keegan, Marsh, Gascoigne, Beckham, Francis Lee, Francis, Woodcock

Second option answer: Bobby Charlton, Bobby Charlton, Bobby Charlton, Ralph Coates, Bobby Charlton, Bobby Charlton, Chris Kamara, Bobby Charlton, Bobby Charlton, Bobby Charlton, Bobby Charlton,

Which is the only football name in which no letter can be filled in with a pen?

Answer: Hull City

In 1953, four Blackpool players played for England

Answer: Taylor, Matthews, Mortensen and Johnston

Which two Australians won the European Cup with Liverpool?

Answer: Craig Johnston and Harry Kewell

Name three players to join Bolton from Real Madrid;

Answer: Ivan Campo, Nicolas Anelka and Fernando Hierro and is it just us that look at Campo and think of Harpo??

Why did three players join Bolton from Real Madrid?

Answer: Not a clue

Wayne Rooney scored a hat-trick on his Manchester United debut. Against who?

Answer: Fenerbahce of Turkey

Footynotes

The Ultimate Countdown of Footy Trivia